CW00798591

73

Floating,
Brilliant,
Gone

ᘓ

Poems by Franny Choi

Write Bloody Publishing
America's Independent Press

Austin, TX

WRITEBLOODY.COM

Floating, Brilliant, Gone

Choi, Franny
First edition
ISBN: 978-1938912436

Cover art by Jess X. Chen
Proofread by Kelly Frances Porter
Edited by Derrick Brown, Laura Brown-Lavoie, Aaron Samuels
Interior illustrations by Jess X. Chen
Interior layout by Ashley Siebels

Type set in Bergamo from www.theleagueofmoveabletype.com

Printed in Tennessee, USA

Write Bloody Publishing
Austin, TX
Support Independent Presses
writebloody.com

To contact the author, send an email to writebloody@gmail.com

MADE IN THE USA

FLOATING, BRILLIANT, GONE

For Arun, the Nest, & Willie.

FLOATING, BRILLIANT, GONE

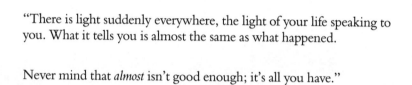

"There is light suddenly everywhere, the light of your life speaking to you. What it tells you is almost the same as what happened.

Never mind that *almost* isn't good enough; it's all you have."

— from *Edinburgh*, by Alexander Chee

NOTES ON THE EXISTENCE OF GHOSTS

Leaves stained onto the sidewalk from yesterday's storm create gray-green watermarks on the pavement, like the negatives of pressed flowers, or the ghost of a letterpress still whispering up from the page. A sidewalk is a haunted thing.

—

I understand the gravity of a train from the empty space and afterbirth air I encounter when I run down to the platform twenty seconds too late. It is the same with all things of such weight – to know them best when you have just missed them.

—

Snow angels; the power of an outline to name an absence holy, a finger pointing to the inherent fiction of angels and therefore haunting.

—

If the stars have, as they say, been dead for millions of years by the time their light reaches us, then it follows that my retinas are a truer thing to call sky.

—

Dove collides into window, leaving a white imprint of its body.
A crime scene outline saying, *Take this, the dust of me. Remember the way my body was round and would not move through glass.*

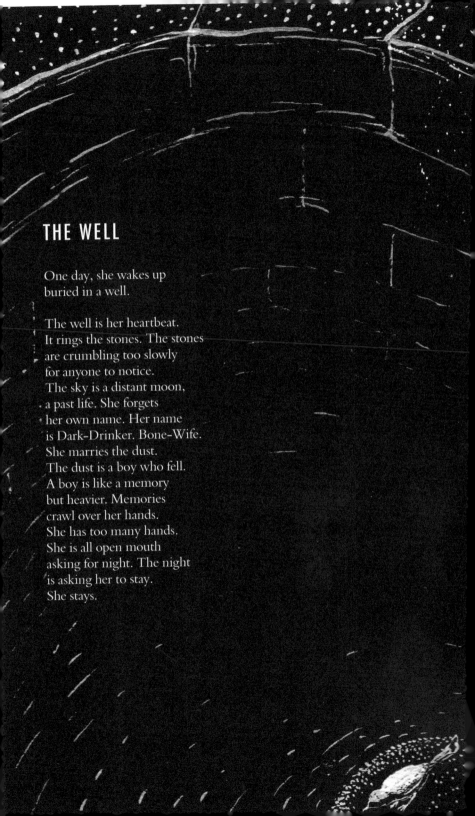

THE WELL

One day, she wakes up
buried in a well.

The well is her heartbeat.
It rings the stones. The stones
are crumbling too slowly
for anyone to notice.
The sky is a distant moon,
a past life. She forgets
her own name. Her name
is Dark-Drinker. Bone-Wife.
She marries the dust.
The dust is a boy who fell.
A boy is like a memory
but heavier. Memories
crawl over her hands.
She has too many hands.
She is all open mouth
asking for night. The night
is asking her to stay.
She stays.

HALLOWEEN, 2009

When my boyfriend's mother
called to tell me

he was dead
I called her a liar

and took the day off.
That night, I got ready

for the reading of my play —
washed my face,

put up my hair,
and changed: black shirt,

black pants. Everyone
told me I looked

like a writer.

FIRST BLOOD AFTER

Hallelujah. The sheets
are stained with *not*.

Organs exhale their verdict
and here, in the sliding weight

of morning, it starts to seep
away. Now the last threat

of a family darkens
softly behind my hip bones.

Now I begin the washing
and the learning to be new. Now

I try not to wait for him
to come home.

SPEAKING PRACTICE

Today our Korean teacher asked us
what year we would rewind to
if we had the choice.

The secret
skipped a beat, leaped
straight into my mouth
        but this tongue
           is an old pocket watch
           a rusty heirloom.

Later, alone,
I answered:

You are asking
if I would rather know or
forget. If I would give
all of this up in order to be
                    happy. Yes. It is
important to be happy. Yes.
I would go back to holding him
and not knowing.

ANNIE MASON'S COLLIE

was the first death she watched.
In the kitchen
the dog lifted its head
before its body emptied
quiet as a sink.

I've never seen death
streak across the sky
of a loved one's face –
just mapped out the craters it leaves

stayed up with dreams
of its explode and
howl and nothing
clogging my eyes. I am

lucky.

      Annie married
her letter jacket love
last winter. Sometimes it all
works out. I kept the invitation
on my dresser for months.

Let it curl
first into bark   then ash.

MUD

I walked through the first boy like a pool of water churning with living things, fetal creatures that recognized me from when I floated upside down in the dark. I could see my face reflected in him but was distracted by the storm below, many-legged secrets calling themselves by my name. *The universe doesn't speak to me anymore*, he said, *it just mutters under its breath once in a while.* The boy who taught me to believe in omens began to smell like an old pond, fish bones bubbling to the surface.

So I waded back out, still wet of him, too afraid to wring him out of my clothes in case I was wrong.

—

I walked through the second boy like a garden, a place to close the gate, away from the crashing symphonies of the city. We disappeared among the cabbages, each leaf waxy and familiar as our mothers' elbows. In the pantry of the earth, everyone thought in the same language, the common bodily knowledge of dirt and sun. But when I passed him a fig of me to sink his teeth into, it dropped with a sound like a long blank stare, and I dug for worms and the howls of writhing things but found only seeds, half-sprouted and too holy between my fingers.

So I walked out, backwards, kissing each bed and leaving the gate open in case he wanted to call me back.

—

I walked into the third boy like a house that had been there all along, wondering how long the porch light had been on when I fell against the doorbell and tumbled in. Now I'm standing in the front hall, tracking mud on the carpet and afraid to touch couches once familiar to my weight. I look for my face among the picture frames, wondering if he'll ever come downstairs,

and whether I want him to find me like this: smelling of compost, covered in algae, dripping pond and garden all over his floor.

SABOTAGE

She is a cat who can't stop coughing up dead things,
hiding them in everyone's shoes, all the teeth
she's swallowed snowballing into wood chippers,
hacking up balls of tangled wire, spiked mirrors,
a still-twitching chicken heart, a broken mug handle,
all the hoarded bottom-drawer shards making friction,
waiting for the wind to turn, for the frog in her stomach
to burst and coat her mouth with its ruin.
Beneath every swallow, always the threat of bile,
always the choice to summon the storms,
to drown the house in her shame and prove
she's too sick to be brought inside.

KIMCHI

My parents' love for each other
was pickled in the brine of 1980,
spent two decades fermenting

in an air-tight promise.
Their occasional salt caught
a slow fever, began to taste like

a buried secret. They choked
in each other's vinegar, dug for pockets
of fresh-cut love, once green and whole,

now a shrunken head, floating.
Every night, she pulls it, messy and
barehanded, out of the jar, slices it

into slivers, and we all swallow,
smiling through the acrid burden
kicking in our throats.

NATIVE LANGUAGE

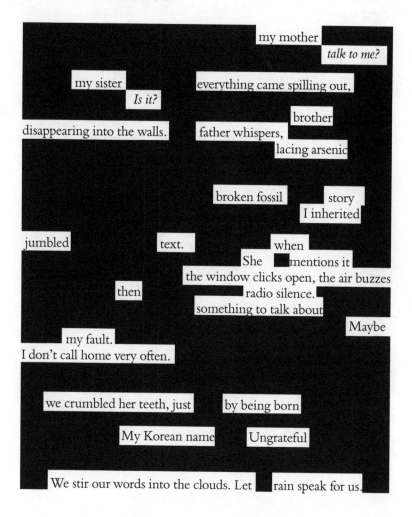

my mother

talk to me?

my sister

Is it?

everything came spilling out,

brother

disappearing into the walls.   father whispers,

lacing arsenic

broken fossil   story

I inherited

jumbled   text.   when

She   mentions it

the window clicks open, the air buzzes

then   radio silence.

something to talk about

Maybe

my fault.

I don't call home very often.

we crumbled her teeth, just   by being born

My Korean name   Ungrateful

We stir our words into the clouds. Let   rain speak for us.

REAL TALK
after Fatimah Asghar

My lover:	What's wrong?
Me:	My family tree is a wreath on a fishing line.
My lover:	Are you okay?
Me:	There's a tree trunk stuck in my throat. Roots disguising themselves as blood vessels, and all that. I'm all sap.
My lover:	Can you say that again?
Me:	I drank too much sun. The stars are making a bell tower of my stomach. I think one got caught on its way down. It flares up when there's a storm coming.
My lover:	Do you want to go home?
Me:	For four years, I flew across the ocean every night to press my mouth against a florid reef, a rotting hoof.
My lover:	Are you tired?
Me:	Seven wars, and you're still calling me in for supper, afraid of what the playground will do to my knees. What do you take my apron for? Can't you see I'm a butcher's daughter?
My lover:	Do you want to talk about it?
Me:	Not everything floats. I am trying to learn which parts of me to let sink.

My lover: Do you want me to apologize?

Me: The last time it stormed, I sent my love letters up on a kite string, hung all my keys to the tail. The lightning hit the persimmon tree outside my parents' house instead. They used the wood to build a bed no one sleeps in.

My lover: What do you want?

Me: I don't remember the last time I saw him, only that we rode the train together to Boston, and on the ride home, I knew I was supposed to cry.

My lover: Why didn't you say so?

Me: There is no such thing as grace, only silence.

HOW TO WIN AN ARGUMENT

When he laughs at the texture of your sadness,
turn away from his mouth, no matter how soft.

When he rests his hands on your belly
reach into the coals of your stomach.
Use your brittle to blow a glass nightlight.
Project your blurry colors onto the walls; be proud
of your tiny furnace blinking in the dark.

When he stays quiet as a basement
watch the bulb burn a hole through your palm
and shatter on the floor. When he disappears

behind you, free fall into miles of sleepless. Be cast
into night. Be spark in the wind – floating
and brilliant and gone.

When you shrug his body off you, let him stroke your spine,
try to shudder you back open. Let him reach
toward your light, call you
back. Let him try.

Then, blow out the candle
in your window. Let him
mourn you.

THE HINDSIGHT OCTOPUS

HABITAT:
Northern Atlantic Ocean caves and Greyhound luggage compartments; often several miles from the nearest ATM.

DIET:
Omnivorous. Common prey include missed appointments, mistakenly sent text messages, unsuccessful jokes, wrong turns, right turns that look wrong for the first few blocks, and all manners of small errors.

BEHAVIOR:
The Hindsight Octopus is most notable for its ability to latch onto mistakes and insecurities with a vise-like grip. When hunting, the octopus will seize its prey with its powerful tentacles and continue to tighten its grip until it faints from exhaustion. The Hindsight Octopus often stalks the ocean floor alone or retreats to its cave after feeding. It has been discovered that the octopus's output of ink increases after these hunts. It is only after reenacting each moment several times through elaborate displays of ink that the Hindsight Octopus is able to lay the skeleton of its prey to rest in the garden surrounding its cave. Though this animal is widely known for its "performances," scientists disagree as to whether this behavior is beneficial to the creature, or a debilitating evolutionary fluke.

DID YOU KNOW?
The only way to kill a Hindsight Octopus is to release it into the wild.

WARNING

in my dream   wet as an oil spill   i sweat drops
of you   speak in fever tongues   tape pearling
at my mouth   sticky aphrodisiac pulling

the skin from my lips   i blow you kisses
like fly paper   in return   you blow honeyed
harpoons into my ears   sharp nothings that

spin in my head til i'm buzzing & blurry as
a ceiling fan
                        & you're the eye of the storm
a poised fork   stalking the whites of my eyes

ORIENTALISM (PART I)

What wouldn't you do
to be held? Don't tell me
you've never taped shut
your own mouth.

There are many ways to hold water
without being called a vase.
To drink all the history
until it is your only song.

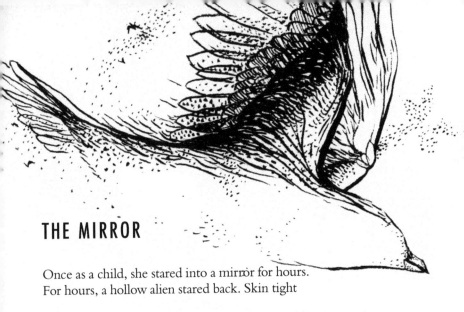

THE MIRROR

Once as a child, she stared into a mirror for hours.
For hours, a hollow alien stared back. Skin tight

over bone over eyes, a hide to dry
in the sun. *Who are you,* she mouthed.

Who are you who are you who are you
echoed the stranger a half-step ahead.

She said, *I am,* but already the other
was warbling, *I am iamiamiamiam*

and she said, *Go back to where you came from*
and the alien was laughing and laughing and tears

sailed down, down the glass because
she could not recognize her own memories,

her own memories from the colors painted
in her skin, in the glass, in her skin.

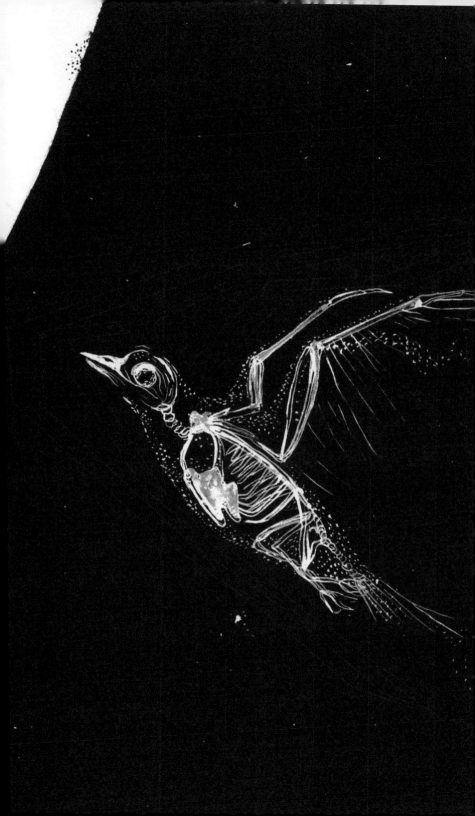

BIRD WATCHING

I.

Look. She's fallen
onto the curb of the corner store,
a goose shot from the sky.

See the crooked haunting her mouth,
limbs splintered into strange angles; makeup
bleeding watercolors; eyes hollow
as her bones.

She could be an angel whose wings
burned off in the atmosphere –
an exquisite waste.

II.

Everyone loves
a dead girl.

Everyone drools when the virgin falls
into the gnarled jaws
of the earth – red mouth cut slack,
eyes empty. Everyone wants
a broken-glass girl,
bought second hand.

Look. The damage
was already there.

CHINKY
after Rachel McKibbens

I. LETTER FROM THE WORLD TO MY EYES

How'd you get so slice?
Razor pinch all flat-like? All puff
& sting? What's your allergy?
Hi bucktooth cartoon. Hi war
paddy. Hi refugee. Spit. Take it.
Tight lids. Dagger flick. Stick
shift. Tease. Lemon juice.
Wide screen. We all scream.
What are you mad? Seething in
the corner? Cat squeezing
fish spine from back? What are you
blind-eye? What are you cock-
roach? What are you gleaming
all teeth no iris at the sun's grin?

II. LETTER FROM MY EYES TO THE WORLD

Act like you've

never seen a pinhole

camera. I drink every

every. Condense light

into its smallest body,

skin it alive.

TO THE MAN WHO SHOUTED "I LIKE PORK FRIED RICE" AT ME ON THE STREET

you want to eat
me — out
of these jeans & into
something a little
cheaper. more digestible.
more bite-sized. more

come: i'm greasy for you.
slick my hair with MSG every morning.
i'm bad for you. red-light district
stuck in your teeth. taste like
a takeout box between
my legs. taste like dried squid.
lips puffy with salt. brimming
with foreign.

so call me
pork: curly-tailed obscenity
been playing in the mud. dirty meat.
worms in your stomach. give you
a fever. dead meat. butchered girl
chopped up & cradled in styrofoam
for you — candid cannibal.
want me bite-sized
no eyes to clog your throat.

but i've been watching
from the slaughterhouse
ever since you named me
edible. think you're
the first to sit at this
table? to ask for a cookie

at the end? call yourself
lucky. chef.
archaeologist – any name
to thicken your jaw.

then listen
for my sow squeal
scream murder in molars.
feel salt awaken
my synapses. watch me kick
back to life. tentacles
& teeth. resurrected electric.
revenge—squirming alive
in your mouth
strangling you quiet
from the inside out.

SECOND MOUTH

Other-lips whispering between her legs
What they called black hole   not-thing
is really packed full of secrets   A rebel mouth

testifying from the underside   Careful
not to let it speak too loudly Only hum
demure   in polite company   never laugh

or spit on the sidewalk   or complain
lest we both be dragged under the wheels of
one of those   Or worse   coddled

smiled at   as at a lap dog acting wolf
Or worse called ugly a cruel joke   Or
    there are always worse things

Too many messengers shot   But then
who wouldn't fear an eyeless face
whose ghost stories always come true?

PUSSY MONSTER

from Lil' Wayne's "Pussy Monster," rearranged in order of frequency

for flu food bowl stood no more soup remove spoon drink juice salt
pepper heard well cool job blow bet mic check how don't have clue but
find show tell lift top lip smell swallow spit every time goes get call
Dracula vacuum catfish fish cat tuna smack flip spatula lil runnin so
tackle baby be worm apple butt go backin front throw black Acura been
this game actress told action cameras lookin hope yeah where know
rain hurricane imagine did pearl talk jump here hi taste taste what what
cold cold suck suck hot hot blew blew there there one one two two
still still put put face face reason reason why why mama mama need need
stay stay gotta gotta survive survive let let up up throw throw on on
words words better better comin comin could could tongue tongue with
with over over over out out out she she she eat eat eat feed feed feed
walk walk walk got got got wanna wanna wanna make make make
make do do do do your your your your just just just just when when
when when in in in in if if if if can can can can I'ma I'ma I'ma I'ma it's
it's it's it's I'm I'm I'm I'm alive alive alive alive of of of of of cause
cause cause cause cause now now now now now her her her her her
I'll I'll I'll I'll I'll like like like like like like a a a a a a a that that that that
that that that that girl girl girl girl girl girl girl girl girl my my my my
my my my my my monster monster monster monster monster
monster monster monster monster to to to to to to to to to to to to
and and and and and and and and and and and and and it it it it it it it
it it it it it it me me me me me me me me me me me me me me the the
the the the the the the the the the the the the the the the the the the you
you you you you you you you you you you you you you you you you you
you you you you you I I I I I I I I I I I I I I I I I I I I I I I I I I I I I I la la la la
la la la la la la la la la la la la la la la la la la la la la la la la la la la la la
la pussy pussy pussy pussy pussy pussy pussy pussy pussy pussy pussy
pussy pussy pussy pussy pussy pussy pussy pussy pussy pussy pussy
pussy pussy pussy pussy pussy pussy pussy pussy pussy pussy
pussy pussy pussy pussy pussy pussy pussy

JUST LIKE A WOMAN OR, GIRLS ARE LIKE PEOPLE EXCEPT THEY DON'T HAVE DICKS

say it like
a woman (everything other
than single-stroke sky-scraper
sword-smiting quick-chop logic):

every maybe/never word i say
is true; & felt; real; violent;
honey slow burning
                       — where's
the sentence in that? i am not
single-stroke 1 so i must be
zero / one-less / no-one –

no; there is nothing hollow about me.
we are not symbols, though we do
crash brass. all ways of sound & pulse
& woman. i'm a woman named *always*
kissing herself; rain on the ocean;
subject & object; rubbing my own
legs; making my own sentences;
like a woman; like dark chocolate
furnace; late-summer laughter;
hills searing the sky; fog;
amphetamine; pearls; night
holding the trees close; so *please*

don't let on that you knew me when
i was hungry and it was your world.

ODE TO MY ARMPIT HAIRS

O, Armpit Hairs! You gnarled trees hunchbacking
towards the sun! You brave umpteen fallen soldiers!
You weeds conspiring beneath the porch!
For so long, I hardly let you poke your heads
above ground before sending you to the gutter,
even during the months you were safely gagged
beneath miles of wool. For so long, I thought myself
a rich douchebag's gardener – or else, hummed
India Arie and ignored your steady march,
claimed *liberated* but secretly called myself
a negligent housewife.   O!, Armpit Hairs.
Even lying beside a militant feminist, I
recruited your absence to help me play woman.

But now – ! You flawless undergrowth! You
fantastic vacant lot run wild! You precisely
scattered unfurl! I am sending up
three cannon shots and a brass fanfare
as you sail
                    to the shower floor. Let this
soapy river captain carry you on to your next
great adventure. O, dandelion scraggle!
I wish you miles of shapeshift, clean boot straps,
and wet soil to stretch your impossible legs.

PACKING INSTRUCTIONS
an introduction to drag kinging

Sling low, sweet chariot. Make way, clear the roads of your pant legs for this new presence, thy kingdom come. Make way in BVDs, pocketed briefs, banana hammocks, blackboard and charcoal with cupped palms to catch hanging fistfuls of clay. Dildos provide rubber function at the ready, potential energy sparking secretly. Stuffed condoms give another approximation, being designed to wrap around the referent on other bodies. But never underestimate the power of a rolled-up sock. Even this heart-sized, cotton thing will feel new between your legs. You will find yourself holding it, like an amateur thief's fingers fluttering to his pocket at a loud noise.

Press it up against your mattress. Remember her quick breath in, lips parting into her shoulder. Remember this as you pace the room, prowl the sidewalk, cross the stage. Feel it hanging, shifting with each step, strapped tight into shorts. Armed and ready, standing at attention. It will rub back and forth, feel at first like something to try to step over and fold into your crotch, like a borrowed maxi pad.

But soon, you will find it affecting your walk, longer lunges that land like declarative sentences. Make way, clear the streets. You will find your pelvis stretch wider as it remembers cowboys in cigarette jeans astride leather saddles. Thy kingdom come. Swagger forward, dipping with every other step, heel-toe. Lope with thick lines, a coughing pickup truck, more shoulder than hip, more engine than oven. Drive into the spotlight and stand on sturdy beams. Grab the bulge and hear the high-pitched screams from long-haired women, slender arms in the air flailing for you. Catch the kisses and catcalls with a snarling nod. You are steel and broad shoulders. You are sleek snaps and gliding punches. You are swing and knuckle and hard.

You are a marvel.

HOW TO GET HOME SAFELY

When late
when walking alone
keep fingers tight
around keys. Be lined
with teeth -- anything
but soft. Name
every tire screech
dinner bell. Every
voice *auctioneer.* Be
poison – shadow
and sharp at once.
Hear footsteps. Be
quick-draw. Let static
pound in ears until –

the click of heels
loosens your fists.
Then be minefield
rusting in the rain.

When you arrive at your stoop
unattacked again, let the smoke
soot everything inside you.
Let your bubbling fear spill
over the sides, not quite sexy enough
to be called *survivor's guilt.*

Instead, call it a siren, a hungry cat,
anything that's learned
to imitate a crying child
to get what it needs.

BAIT

We've brought our friend Emilio back to his apartment
after finding him sloshing down Manton,
a raft in an unseen storm. He is spilling over the lid

but still wants to go to the party. He is smiling with every tooth
at the darkening night that we know is all around him these days.
We try to coax him back from the gangplank. He is still laughing,

the deck pitching his body like a whale juggling its prey.
We are still trying to smile, crooning calm waters
when Emilio reaches out, hooks his fingers into my scalp –

Chinita, chinita bella
                                    before he is pulled down.

Then he is in bed. Then we are driving away,
unsure of how to apologize to each other.

I can't touch anyone without crying, so I look out the window,
let the trees play back the memory of tentacles in my hair,
how small I made myself, how I pleaded quiet as a bird

knocked out of the air. How the dog knows why it's kicked,
declawed by what it calls *friend*. How I'd seen the clouds
gathering in his eyes just before he hit the water, and how

I know that storm all too well, the secret
always swimming beneath the surface
of every grinning ally.

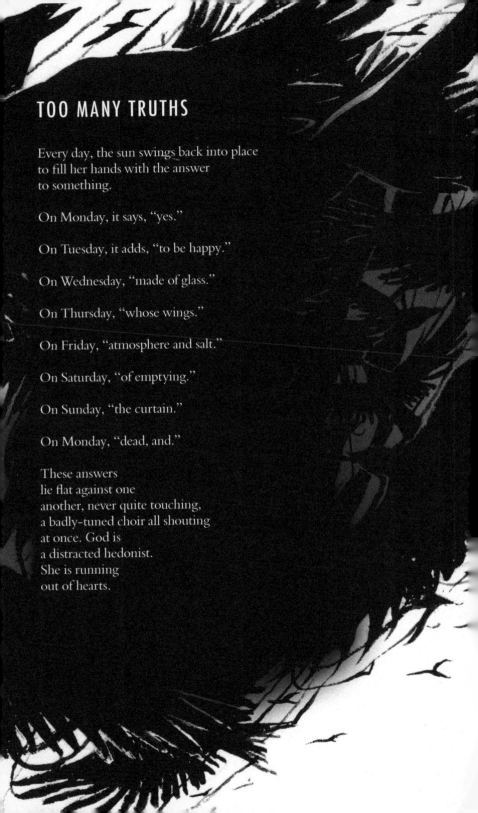

TOO MANY TRUTHS

Every day, the sun swings back into place
to fill her hands with the answer
to something.

On Monday, it says, "yes."

On Tuesday, it adds, "to be happy."

On Wednesday, "made of glass."

On Thursday, "whose wings."

On Friday, "atmosphere and salt."

On Saturday, "of emptying."

On Sunday, "the curtain."

On Monday, "dead, and."

These answers
lie flat against one
another, never quite touching,
a badly-tuned choir all shouting
at once. God is
a distracted hedonist.
She is running
out of hearts.

GENTRIFIER

the new grocery sells *real* cheese, edging out
    the plastic bodega substitute. the new neighbors

know how to feed their children, treat themselves
    to oysters sometimes. other times, to brunch. *finally,*

some good pastrami around these parts. new cafe
    on broadway. new trees in the sidewalk. everyone

can breathe a little easier. neighborhood association
    throws a block party. builds a dog park right

in the middle of the baseball field. crime watch listserv
    snaps photos of suspicious natives. *how'd all these ghosts*

get in my yard? cop on speed dial. arrange flowers
    as the radio croons orders. rubber on tar,

skin on steel. an army of macbook pros guarding
    its french presses. revival pioneers. meanwhile,

white college grads curse their racist neighbors,
    get drunk at olneyville warehouse punk shows,

ride their bikes on the right side of the road, say *west end*
    like a badge, while folks on the other side of cranston street

shake their heads and laugh. interrogation lamps
    burning down their stoops. banks gutting their houses.

i look more like the cambodian kids against that wall
    than any of my roommates. but feel safest within two miles

of an espresso machine. look around at parties and think,
    fresh saplings. revival pioneers. know folks look at me

on my bike and think, *ivy league. dog park. treat yourself*
    to a neighborhood sometimes. none of this land is mine

but our footprints are everywhere. silent battlefront
    we new settlers shove into our back pockets,

lump in our collective throat as we chase a new world,
    sweep the foyer, promise we'll help clean up the mess.

TOO MANY TRUTHS

I'm in love with a broken
glass. I'm in love with a broken
city. I'm in love with a city shuddering
at my feet. What I mean is there was
a man on the ground at the bus station.
What I mean is I didn't give my seat
to an old woman once. What I mean is
sometimes I have a seat and others don't.
One time I fell in love with people
called other. One time I tried
my hardest and I still got laid off.
Everyone was so sorry. I'm sorry
for being on the other side.
One time a white man
yelled about how sorry he was
for being white. One time I fell in love
with a white man. One time I lost
a different man. One time I
lost a woman too, but different.
One time a different woman
built my body inside her body.
Then my body left hers.
Then pockmarked body then body riddled
with jokes then body tried to hide.
Body left home and rode off toward
college. Body studied anything it wanted.
Body looked at bodies at the bottom
of a hill. Body loved and loved
but wouldn't come down. Body called

itself Master. Body named itself Free.
Body bought its own freedom. Body sold
itself to the top. Body broken glass all by itself.
Body spills all the light. Body
all the light. Body only dark
when it wants to be.

THE MANTIS SHRIMP SPEAKS

The Mantis Shrimp is a small crustacean that can see more colors than any other animal. It can also deliver a blow equivalent to the force of a bullet and has been known to crack aquarium glass.

It's hard, being a prism in a burning city.

When the photoreceptors of my fear flare up, I see every possible shade of truth refract out from each speck of word floating in the wind, and I am filled with a need to crack the looking glass between my jaws. Sometimes, the world is six times more vibrant than I have the patience for, every outline electric and multiplicitous. Text / subtext / historical ripples / every television ad a screaming rainbow bursting with parallel deaths. Can't you see? This moment is all colors imaginable.

This is the only way I know how to tell someone what I want, to describe the infinitely unfolded accordion of my heart. To love with a rage gone blind from the knowledge of the stolen lands, dirty wars, honor killings, false idols, forced soldiers, and buried throats haunting every sentence. Too many truths setting my retinas ablaze, and me mad, mad, mad at the end of it all.

TORNADO

in my dream, i am galloping
on the winds of a violent revolution, stretching
straight letter I, a storm of churning
voices collected into a single
spine. i am radical rapid
turning, uprooting houses
blasting open government
offices, swarms of solid
atmosphere and salt-
water rising against the
pyramids rearing
on the horizon
blackening out
whole suns
collective
thun
der

        i've never seen
        the file cabinets emptied
        into the streets. only dreamt
        blurry photographs of
        swirling singularity.

        i hear most storms collapse
        back into sand and thin, whipping
        too fast around their own gravity.

        i stand on my steps and watch
        the leaves moving in the wind
        until one is lifted
        into the air and another

carried briefly
                into its surge,
dragonflies colliding and
multiplying, sweet
accidental
              turbine. and it is
a hint;

a fleeting tug
at the corner of a mouth.

ORIENTALISM (PART II)

My cousin and her white boyfriend
dressed as John Lennon and Yoko Ono
for Halloween one year. Déjà vu
got nothing on us yellow girls
find ourselves tangled with white boys.

Our doppelgangers are everywhere.
We hold hands on the sidewalk,
and the prophets roll their eyes.
At the Korean restaurant,
our mirror image is pointing to the menu
and pronouncing everything wrong. I look up
to catch her winking back:

> *Be the beating myth to his tin man chest.*
> *Be sesame oil to his white bread.*

The textbook tarot cards
are snickering dirty secrets again.
In line at the movies, there's another me
pressing against my lover's pale twin,
simpering, dough-eyed babble.
From here, it sounds like:

> *Be manic pixie in the lantern, twinkling sex*
> *pressed against the glass. Let him*
> *run his tongue over your strange land,*
> *taste only honey.*

In the magazine, the only woman
I could possibly be
is spilling from the conqueror's

ropy arms. Her lightless eyes
will not let me sleep:

> *Be the prize slung over his shoulder,*
> *an open bar of middle-shelf kink.*

The more I spit history lessons
at their backs, the faster the acid flies
back into my own face:

> *Bury the boys who look like your brother*
> *and wrap yourself around a picket fence*
> *to whom you will only ever be a dream.*

Each time, my lover
kisses the venom from my cheeks,
presses the crooked limb of his heart
into my balled fists. Until one day, I look up
and see him there, lips nearly singed off,
looking more like himself
than any ghost. He can't speak,
but his palms are saying:

> Please, my love,
> Not every house is haunted.

So I throw open
all my doors and let him in.

In the bathroom, we only take a moment
to smile at our reflection
before we part the curtain in the mirror
and step inside.

MY LOVERS

I.

My dead lover is a splinter throbbing at dusk. A shard of castle rock
frozen in a glass paperweight and doubted. At three in the morning, he
raps his beak against my ear, and I wake up to the drill of silence. My
dead lover is a suitcase of books I left on an eastbound train; a
headlight's afterimage. A starling dying over and over beneath my desk.
A fish hook reeling me to the sun. Four years after he left, he is still
spoon-feeding my heart back into my quivering mouth.

II.

My lover who is here
is here. Freckles
& sweat. Each finger
an encyclopedia of lights
turned on. He is warm
                        and that's
a thousand stars aligned – that this
complicated gathering of flesh
can move and laugh
and make heat.

Under the covers, he is
skin. He is here
and loves me. And
that's the first   and last reason.

THE THREAT OF PEACE

After the rats fled,
the quiet kept her awake
all night.

She panicked:

What if the skeletons stop singing my name?
What if my heart goes deaf?
What if sadness is the secret
to everything?

Then, dawn crept into her room
and the birds sang her to sleep.

DRIVE TO QUINEBAUG VALLEY

Backseat. Shoulder to shoulder. Seatbelts
wedged deep in hips. Honey on my left,
trusted friend on my right. (Who called
the middle seat *bitch*?) Birches whipping
past. Sudden breaks in trees: lakes. Now:
the Scituate Reservoir, no longer myth.
Blessed is the real, this hot meal my love
heated for me. Blessed are the insides of
wrists that wriggle into conversation.
Urgent philosophy in the front seat; here,
only laughter & marveling, the sunlight
skipping across our foreheads. Train car
diners. Roadside antique bazaar. Strange
landscape to our small-city leers. Familiar
shapes – ears and nose that find their way
between jokes.
               Here, a burrowing
place, a chrysalis in the cushions. Safer
than plastic buckles or the promise of
airbags. Safer is this: this heartbeat beside
mine, the ever-rhythm of *live, live, live.*

WHY WE BIKED FORTY MILES TO NARRAGANSETT

There are many reasons – the promise
of water, to offer one example –

but none burns so blood
as the good work of muscles pumping freight
over the earth; as the fact of engine in my knees
and all my lover's inexplicable flesh
churning wind beside me.

The work of love
becomes its own reason; like the heart's
relentless feedback loop, which is infinite
until it isn't; like sweat, being only
(miraculously) itself, and worth it;

like the ocean, having been the ocean
long before we arrived, each wave
newborn and buried at once; like us,
standing breathless at the edge,
astonished by our own lungs.

METAMORPHOSIS

after Nate Marshall

in october, my boyfriend & i
picked apples and dead butterflies
out of a smithfield orchard's
hair. we kissed the dregs of knowledge
from the branches, gathered
the fallen paper monarchs, flat
and brittle as old letters.

                         she told me to call
                         our bed a cocoon.
                         whispered her arms
                         around my new pink.

he held the last raspberry
of the season to my lips.
the sun was shining. everything
was dying & we
laughed hand in hand
over the graves of
tiny kings.

                         for years some new
                         charge had been growing
                         in the back pockets of
                         my heart. quiet & unassuming
                         as a pinecone. strange shapes
                         stirring awake in the gardens
                         of my wet dreams.

the butterflies had migrated
in a giant swarm, somewhere over the

border. across yellow brick checkpoints
& wicked desert, all the way to this
new england orchard where one cold night
wiped out a whole battalion. frail &
mighty, they paid little mind
to the miles of barbed wire history
that stood in the way.

for four months i knew nothing
but the walls of our cave,
sweet musk, skin soft
& brown as wet leaves.
felt the molting in my joints
& knew i was becoming
a new species of beautiful.

metaphorically grandiose,
in my hands the butterflies were
unspeakably ordinary.
two-dimensional ticket stubs
to a miracle unwitnessed.
still, i kissed each one
like an amulet.

when i unraveled
the closet i'd spun
around my heart,
i found myself a fragile
factoid, a flightless thing.

after she left, i peeled
the silken armor from my lips.
outside the chrysalis,
the colors were screaming.
everything

                    was different & i
                    was still an insect scuttling
                    over the ruins of battles
                    i hadn't fought.

sometimes entire libraries
of epic poems land
in your palm as a single
paper-thin sigh. sometimes
it is as simple as love.

                    i loved a woman
                    for four months
                    straight. am still floundering
                    on the wings of *queer.*
                    misquoting someone
                    every time i pin it
                    to my chest; every time
                    i pin myself to the display case.

every year a tree will awake
to find the quietest massacre
tinseling its branches.

i pray to this bloodline of break
& burst & migrate with
every butterfly
kiss i lay against his temple.

                    & why classify
                    each strain of pollen
                    dusting my legs?

this is the plant i have chosen
to fall still in. then perhaps to move,

to die, to wake, to shed,
to migrate, to grow,
to fall still in again
& again
brittle pages in the wind.

because i am & am
not flight.
am & am not worm
blinking at sun
& soft shroud

to crawl from & laugh at

& return to.

& this is not a grave.

& this is not the opposite
of free.

REASONS IT'S IMPORTANT TO REST

Some mornings I wake up to half-dreamt
train cars running amuck between my ears
screaming me to work. Lopsided engines
scatter chug. Rats. Flee the corners
of my consciousness. Go dog Go dog Go.

—

Leaf. Leaf. Haul seed back to hive. Feed
worms. Tick tick on their translucent wails.
Ward off hunter. Pass food, a utilitarian
kiss. Cross-examine each pulse. Border
patrol. I am hive am build am push.

—

The world will never stop being urgent,
high tide at rush hour, dishes crashing
everywhere. Want is a self-fulfilling
prophecy, built to trip over its own feet.
I am always drowning in its hunger.

—

What joy is a half-baked dream? What lark
is a broken camera? What fault in the unborn
astronaut? What never in the sky undoven?
Blue prints buried in the attic dumpster? Why
cross the river if not history?

—

Point A and Point B walk into a bar.
B downs ten shots of whiskey and dies prompt
and proud. A sweeps the floor and whistles in
the background. Becomes landlord of everyone's
secrets – but never learns how not to live.

—

The key to dying is to breathe unconditionally.
I stretch out my hide to catch all the trees
in the world. Let each limb become its own
fairy tale. Come, sun. Lather yourself against
my eyelids. I'll hold all your terrific ugly.

—

Stillness is an accordion: empty unfolding
into pitch. There are answers hiding
in the white noise, in the heartbeat of a house.
Writer, become apostle of the sealed box.
Stop searching the clock's face for your own.

NEVER HERE

When the girl finally learned to say "I," her poems clawed out of her mouth and scattered into the sky like crows. Each one multiplied and became

shadow. They roosted in

flesh - feather and beak. They lived

the walls of every house
she dared live in,
every day she dared live.
Then one day, like a light,

her hair. She brushed
and brushed until

the eyes of her lover.
She prayed for the day

and then
died

forever, lived hunger
and joy and war and
desire. They multiplied
again and again until
they blackened the sky

they burst
into the world

and again
became part
of the
universe's
slow hum.

DÉJÀ VU

outlines of branches at dusk   shush of sand
beneath wheels   blinking constellation of city

dusk at spring familiar always-known   brings me
to the memory of a day a story then too   *you know*

who you look like? i must have dreamt his face once
our passing on the tip of my tongue like salt

sharp & distant   i swear someone's slipped me
the end of this story before   how to cook breakfast

spoon it into each other's palms   a script clear
as rooftops set alight by a sun's dying roar

bone-knowledge the shapes of cheekbones & where
to rest my mouth   heavy in my spine as soil

i blinked alive always-knowing how to love
this way   solid   as a city's silhouette

HOW TO DISAPPEAR

I am in the habit of taking half a step into my own curtains, the outer surface of my face being the inverse of glow-in-the-dark tape onto which the stage hand pours flashlight before the show. I drink greedily from the dark, from places under covers, beneath stacks of notebooks, behind the two-way mirror of makeup.

When such hideouts are unavailable (for instance, at a long dinner with strangers following a small but tragic mistake), there is a reserve of darkness in the rumbling cave I call my body. The method is this: I draw a circle around myself, the radius stretching to my glass of water. This becomes the fence around my field of vision and my fingers. I settle into my own nucleus. I burrow. I speak, but the sound is muffled by the walls of limestone and the slow   dripping.   I am a submarine peeking through the curtains of the waves.   A stowaway in   a suit of armor.   I am an eavesdropping cat on the radiator,   so much paw to groom.   I tell my friends I'm not feeling well   as I plug the opposite of a flashlight

                          into my fuel tank

                                        and   wait.

HEAVEN IS A FAIRLY TALE (& VICE VERSA)

We are all
dutifully practicing
our deaths.

UNWORDS

after all, i owe more to pages and stillness than to time-block
penciling-in, grocery line assembly approval. after all this,
i'm too whirlwinded, the minutes too scattered to speak
single words. what, then, is more right

than to approach the quiet on my knees, palms up, to pool myself
for the unwords that a chair by a window could pour into me?

i sit at dawn's feet, kiss her hem. in return
she fills my lungs with sweet nothing. tells me

it is enough to know you can   never
        know this   here

is enough

NOTES

Kimchi is a traditional Korean side dish made with spicy pickled cabbage.

"Real Talk" is after Fatimah Asghar's "Conversations with God."

"Chinky" is after Rachel McKibbens' "Letter From my Heart to my Brain" and "Letter From my Brain to my Heart."

Manton, Broadway, and Cranston (in "Bait" and "Gentrifier") all refer to streets in Providence, Rhode Island. Olneyville and the West End are Providence neighborhoods undergoing gentrification.

Chinita bella (in "Bait") translates to "pretty Chinese girl."

The first line of "The Mantis Shrimp Speaks" ("It's hard, being a prism in a burning city") is from Fatimah Asghar's poem "In Case of Burning."

The Scituate Reservoir, Narragansett, and Smithfield are all beautiful places in Rhode Island. Quinebaug Valley refers to a community college in Connecticut.

"Metamorphosis" is after Nate Marshall's "Fireworks." The poem makes reference to monarch butterflies, which migrate yearly from Central America to Canada and back. No individual butterfly makes the entire round trip.

For lesson plans, writing prompts, and discussion questions for this book, please visit www.frannychoi.com/curriculum.

ACKNOWLEDGMENTS

Grateful acknowledgment is made to the editors of the following publications, in which these poems first appeared, sometimes in slightly different forms:

Apogee Journal: "Packing Instructions" (as part of the series "Notes from 'A Guide to Drag Kinging'")

CAP Magazine: "The Hindsight Octopus" and "The Mantis Shrimp Speaks"

Courage Anthology: Daring Poems for Gutsy Girls: "First Blood After" and "How to Disappear" (as "On Withdrawing")

Flicker and Spark: A Contemporary Queer Anthology of Spoken Word and Poetry: "First Blood After" (as "Sixth Morning After")

Folio: "Reasons It's Important to Rest"

Gesture Magazine: "The Well," "Sabotage," "The Mirror," "Too Many Truths," and "The Threat of Peace"

Loom: "Notes on the Existence of Ghosts"

PANK: "Mud," "Warning," "Pussy Monster," and the second "Too Many Truths"

Poetry Magazine: "Second Mouth" and "To the Man Who Shouted 'I Like Pork Fried Rice' at Me on the Street"

Radius: "Bird Watching," "Bait," "Chinky"

Tandem: "Kimchi," "Packing Instructions," (as "Packing") and "To the Man Who Shouted 'I Like Pork Fried Rice' at Me on the Street"

Thank you also to the Indiefeed Podcast, which broadcast a version of "Notes on the Existence of Ghosts" in audio form.

THANK YOU

To Derrick Brown and Write Bloody.

To Jess X. Chen, for breathing your wildness into these poems.

To Laura Brown-Lavoie, for the countless rounds of edits, tea, and love. To Aaron Samuels, for your encouragement and thoroughness. You two are the godparents of this book.

To Fatimah Asghar, Nate Marshall, Danez Smith, Jamila Woods, Rick Benjamin, Sam Sax, Jason Bayani, Robbie Q. Telfer, Tess Brown-Lavoie, and Emmett Fitzgerald – for your time, edits, and friendship.

To Rick (again), Chanravy Proeung, and Dulari Tahbildar, for showing me what mentorship looks like. To WORD! and ProvSlam, for helping me grow.

To my friends Hieu Nguyen, Phil Kaye, Sarah Kay, VyVy Trinh, Kate Hadley, David Schwartz, Susan Beaty, Kerry Bergin, Muggs Fogarty, Charlotte Abotsi, Paul Tran, Sydney Peak, and Jared Paul, for keeping me sane and making me whole.

To the Stewarts – Sunita, Tony, and Ravi – for your strength; to Arun, for teaching me so much.

To my family, Brigid, Paul, Umma, and Appa, for your patience and humor. I love you.

To Will, my partner, safe house, best friend. You are the first and last reason.

ABOUT THE AUTHOR

Franny Choi lives in Providence, Rhode Island, where she has spent the last three years working in youth, education, and grassroots organizing spaces. Her poems and stories have appeared in *Poetry, PANK, Folio, Fringe, Apogee, CAP, Radius,* and others. A Pushcart Prize nominee, she has been a finalist at the National Poetry Slam, the Individual World Poetry Slam, and the Women of the World Poetry Slam. Her play *Mask Dances* was staged at Brown University's Writing is Live Festival in 2011. Through Project V.O.I.C.E. and the Providence Poetry Slam, Franny teaches creative writing in classrooms and community centers in her city and across the country. See more at www.frannychoi.com.

ABOUT THE ILLUSTRATOR

Jess X. Chen is a multi-disciplinary poet, filmmaker and eco-feminist artist. She explores the complex and powerful languages created when divergent art forms intersect. She is the co-founder of LoveHoldLetGo, a shadow theater and film collective that has toured the North American continent. Their first play "Silence and the Earth" imagines what the Earth would say to humanity if it hadn't been silenced for it's four billion year old life. You can find more of her work at www.jessxchen.com and www.loveholdletgo.com.

IF YOU LIKE FRANNY CHOI, FRANNY CHOI LIKES

Yarmulkes and Fitted Caps
Aaron Samuels

Racing Hummingbirds
Jeanann Verlee

This Way to the Sugar
Hieu Nguyen

What the Night Demands
Miles Walser

The New Clean
Jon Sands

No Matter the Wreckage
Sarah Kay

Write Bloody Publishing distributes and promotes great books of fiction, poetry, and art every year. We are an independent press dedicated to quality literature and book design, with an office in Austin, TX.

Our employees are authors and artists, so we call ourselves a family. Our design team comes from all over America: modern painters, photographers, and rock album designers create book covers we're proud to be judged by.

We publish and promote 8 to 12 tour-savvy authors per year. We are grass-roots, D.I.Y., bootstrap believers. Pull up a good book and join the family. Support independent authors, artists, and presses.

**Want to know more about Write Bloody books, authors, and events?
Join our mailing list at**

www.writebloody.com

WRITE BLOODY BOOKS

CPSIA information can be obtained
at www.ICGtesting.com
Printed in the USA
FSHW020138190419

9 781938 912436